ESTATE PUB

GUILDFORD · WC

BYFLEET · BISLEY · RIPLEY · COMP'
SHALFORD · MILFORD · GODALMIN(

CW00369529

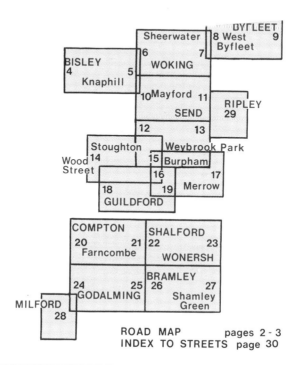

ROAD MAP pages 2 - 3
INDEX TO STREETS page 30

Car Park	P
Public Convenience	C
Place of Worship	+
One-way Street	→
Pedestrianized	▨
Post Office	●

**Scale of street plans 4 inches to 1 mile
Unless otherwise stated**

Street plans prepared and published by ESTATE PUBLICATIONS, Bridewell House, TENTERDEN, KENT
The Publishers acknowledge the co-operation of the local authorities
of towns represented in this atlas.

Ordnance Survey® This product includes mapping data licensed from Ordnance Survey® with the permission of the Controller of Her Majesty's Stationery Office.

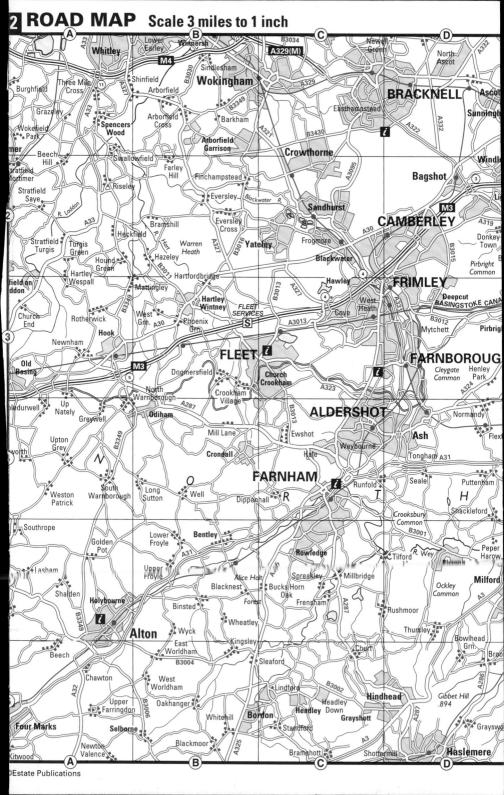

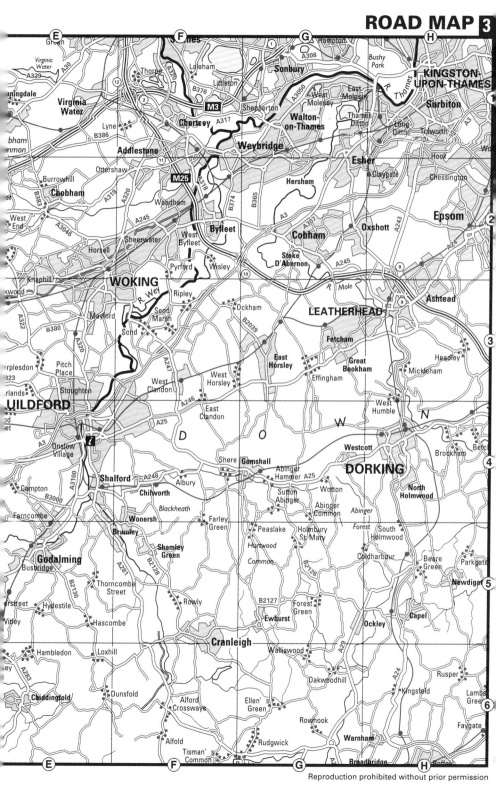

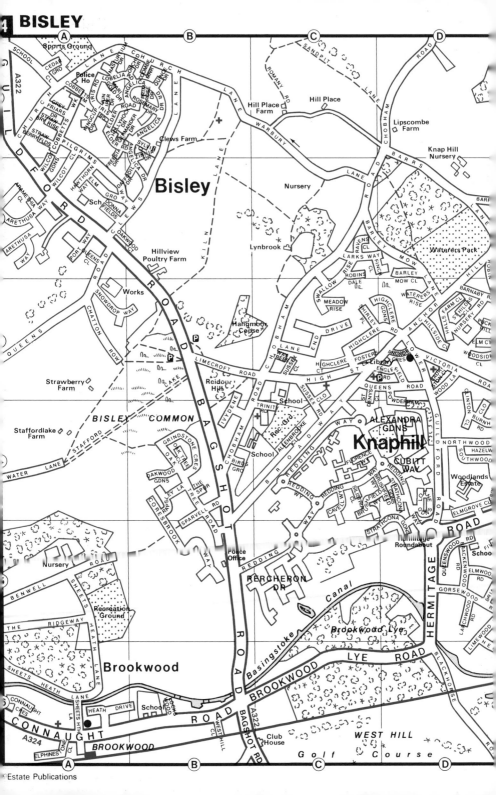

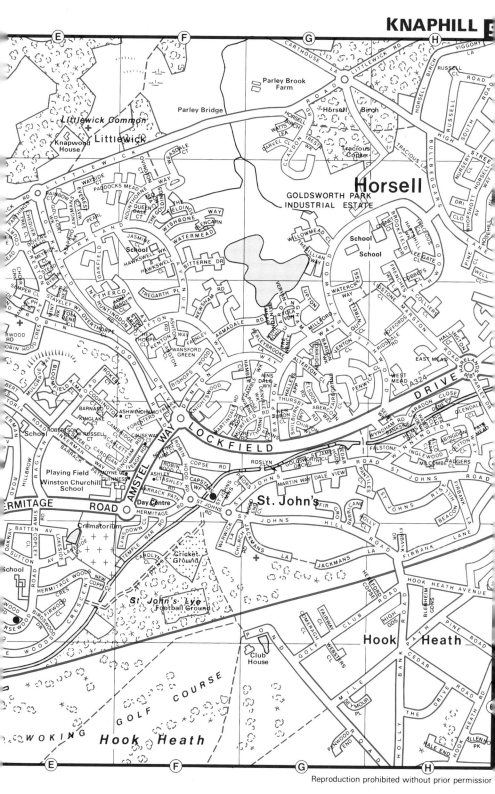

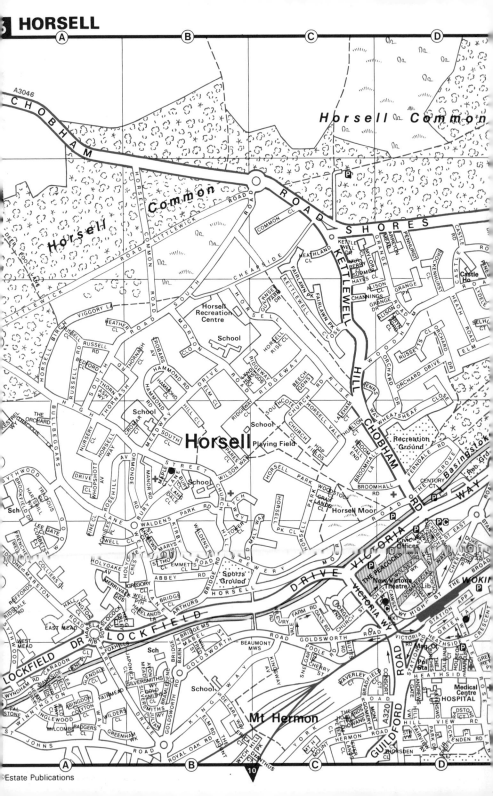

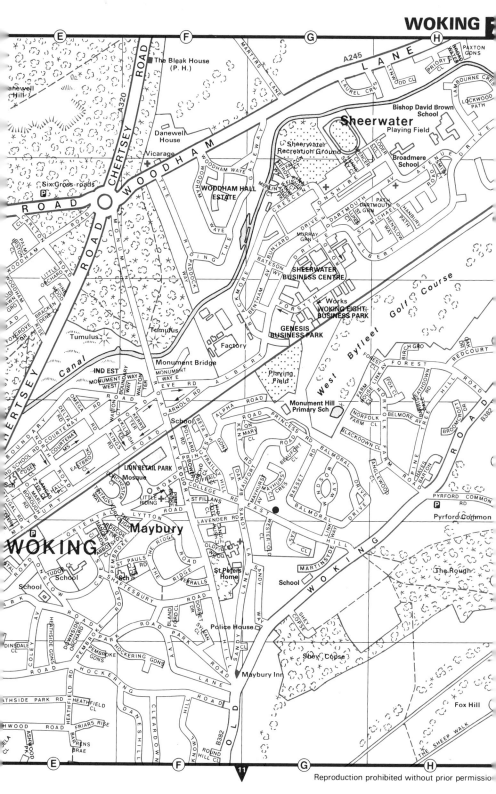

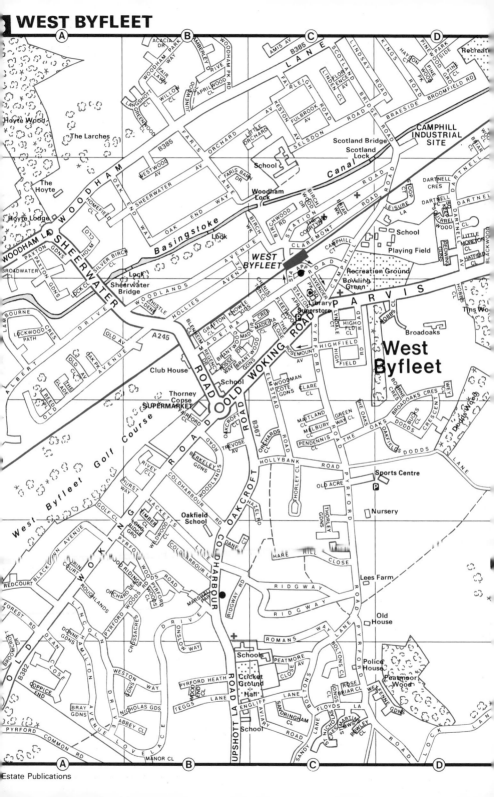

West Byfleet

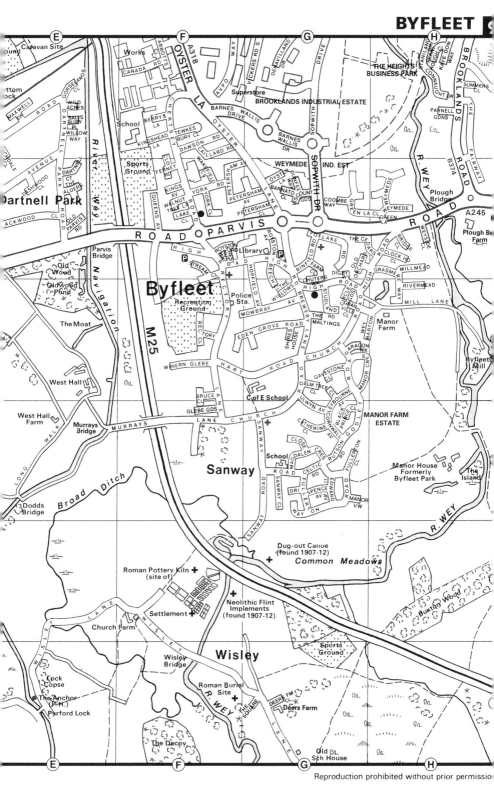

BYFLEET

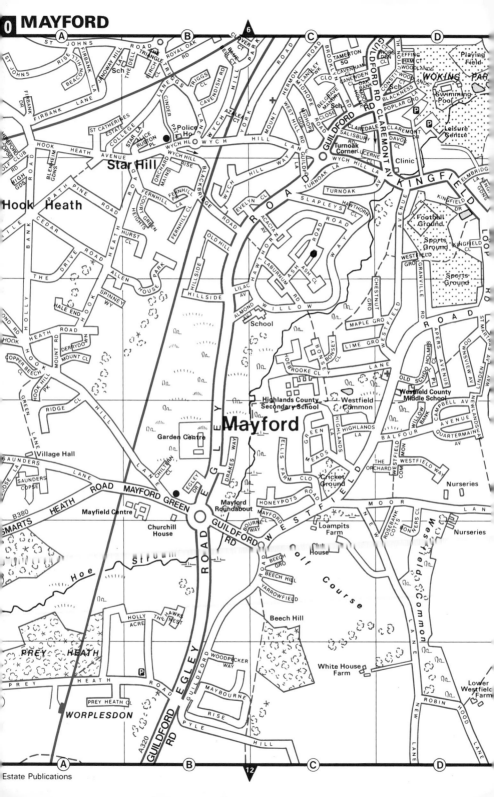

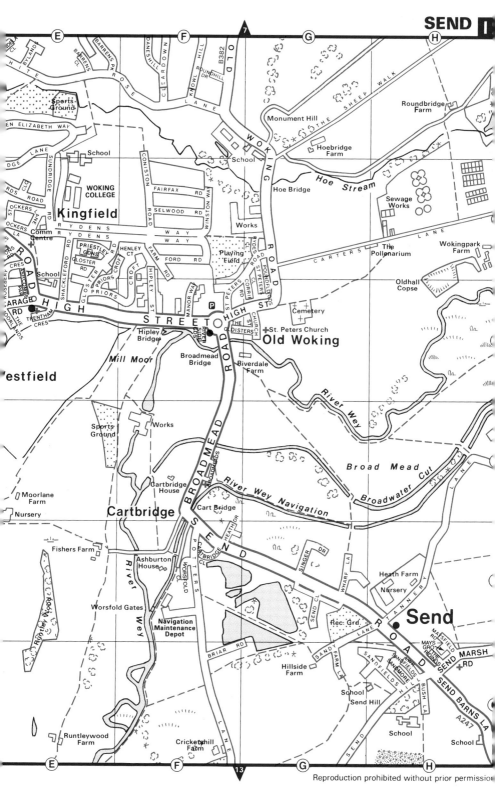

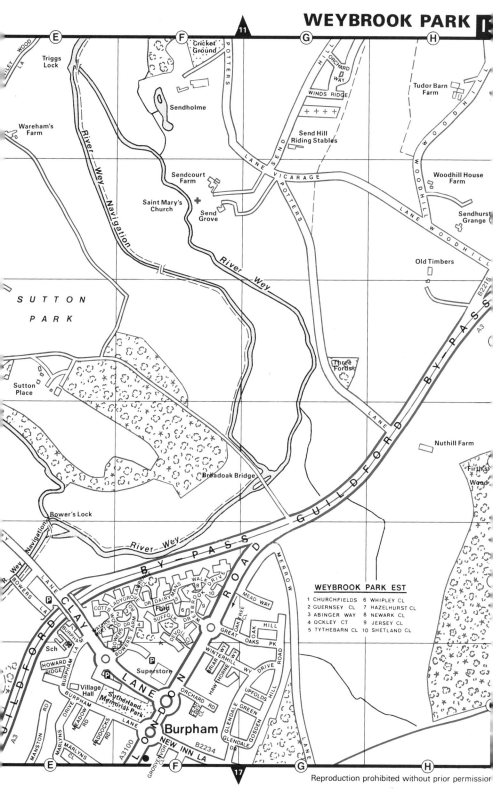

E · F · G · H

WILEY LA · WOOD

Triggs Lock

Cricket Ground

Wareham's Farm

River — Wey — Navigation

Sendholme

Sendcourt Farm

Saint Mary's Church

Send Grove

Orchard Way

Winds Ridge

Tudor Barn Farm

Send Hill Riding Stables

Woodhill House Farm

Sendhurst Grange

Old Timbers

River — Wey

SUTTON PARK

Sutton Place

Three Fords

Nuthill Farm

Broadoak Bridge

GUILDFORD — BY-PASS

Firth's Wood

Bower's Lock

River — Wey

BY-PASS

WEYBROOK PARK EST

1 CHURCHFIELDS	6 WHIPLEY CL
2 GUERNSEY CL	7 HAZELHURST CL
3 ABINGER WAY	8 NEWARK CL
4 OCKLEY CT	9 JERSEY CL
5 TYTHEBARN CL	10 SHETLAND CL

CLAY LANE

LONDON ROAD

MERROW

MEAD WAY

GREAT OAKS

OAK TREE DRIVE

HILL PK

Ford

Suffolk

Sch

HOWARD RIDGE

Superstore

Village Hall

Sutherland Memorial Park

Burpham

WINTERHILL

FRIAR THORNE WY

UPFOLDS HILL DRIVE

GLENDALE GREEN

GOSDEN

ORCHARD RD

MANSTON RD

MARLYNS DRIVE

PADDOCKS RD

NEW INN LA

B2234

GROSVENOR RD

A3100

17

©Estate Publications

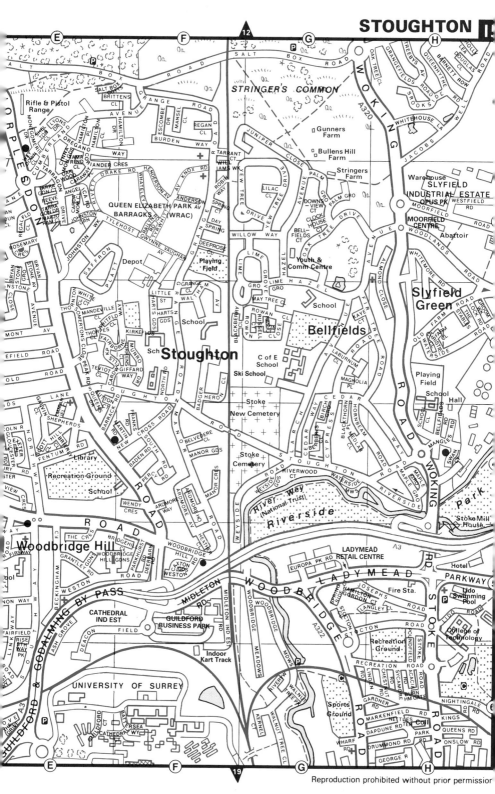

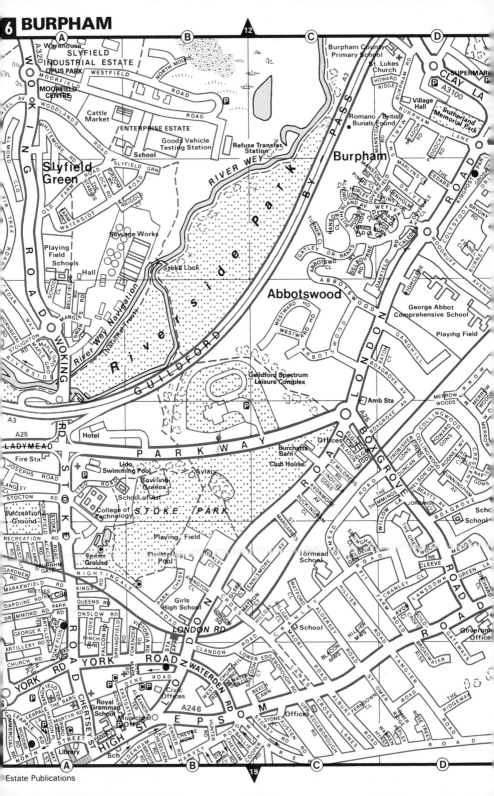

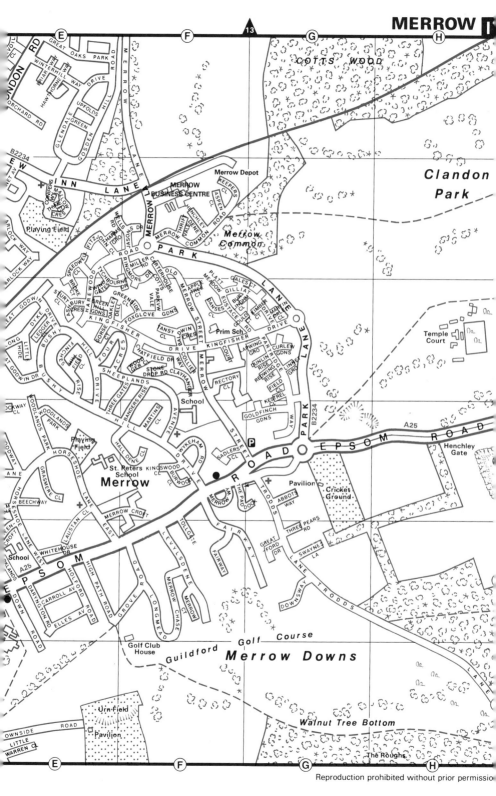

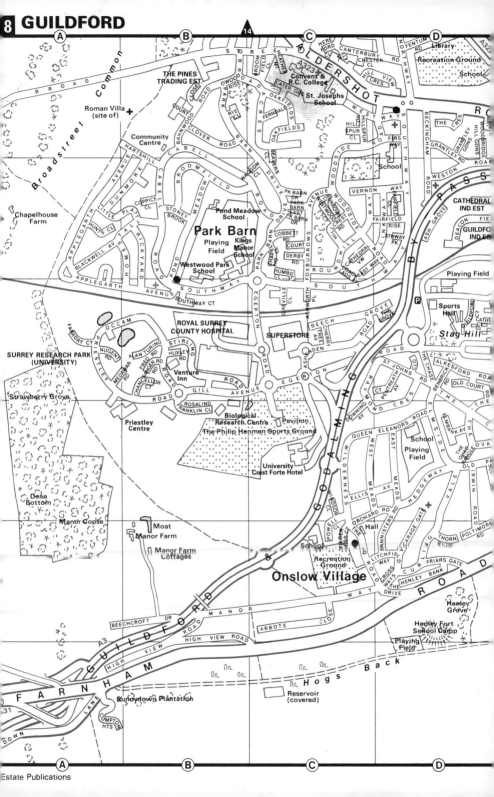

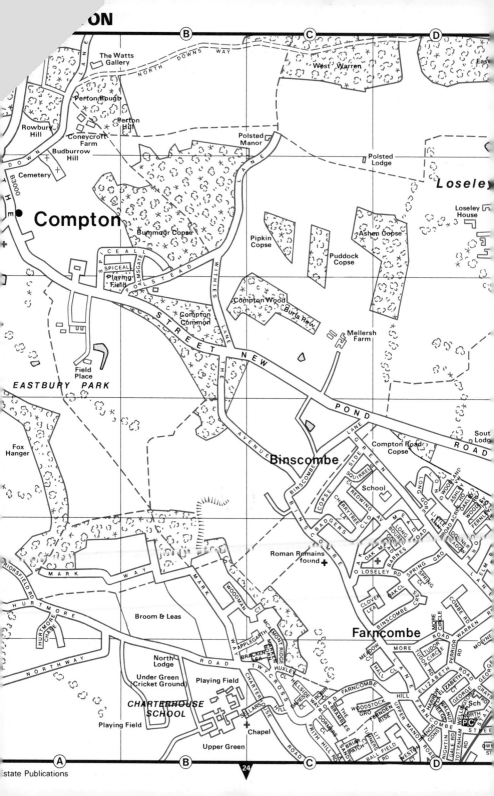

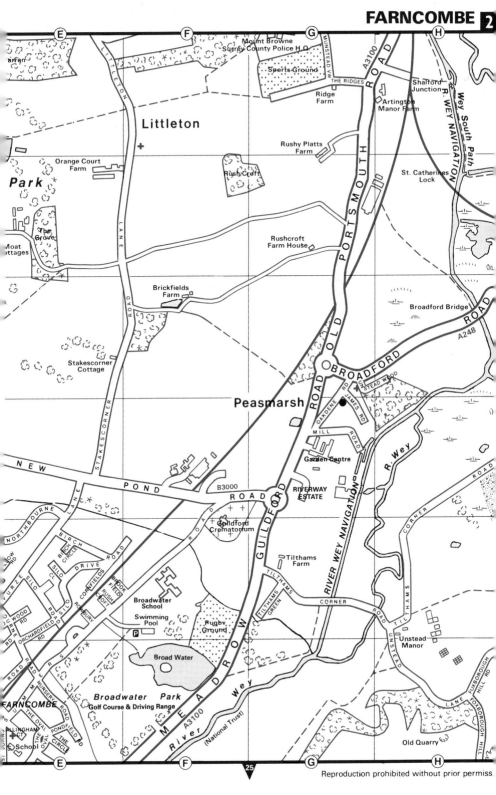

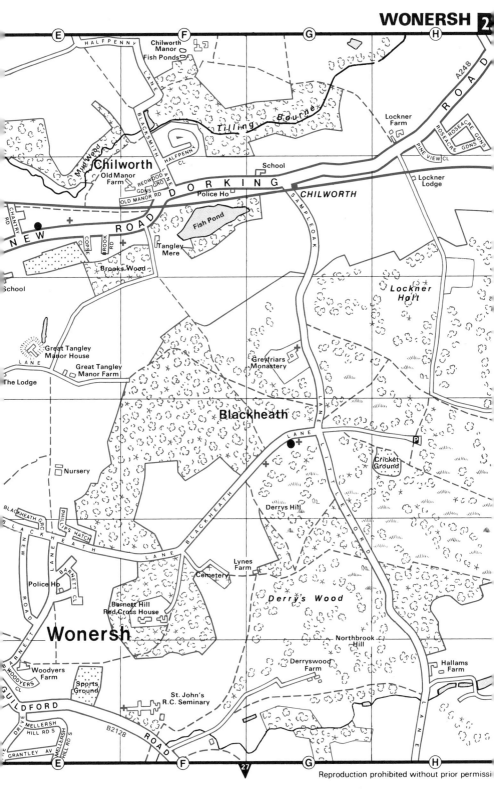

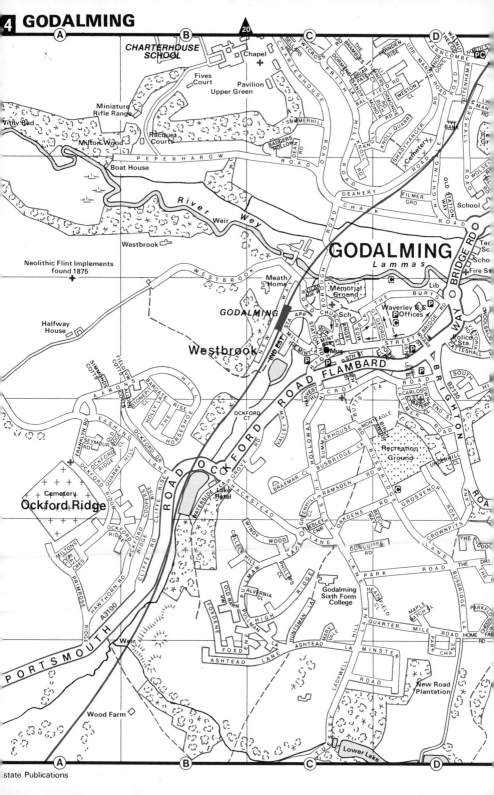

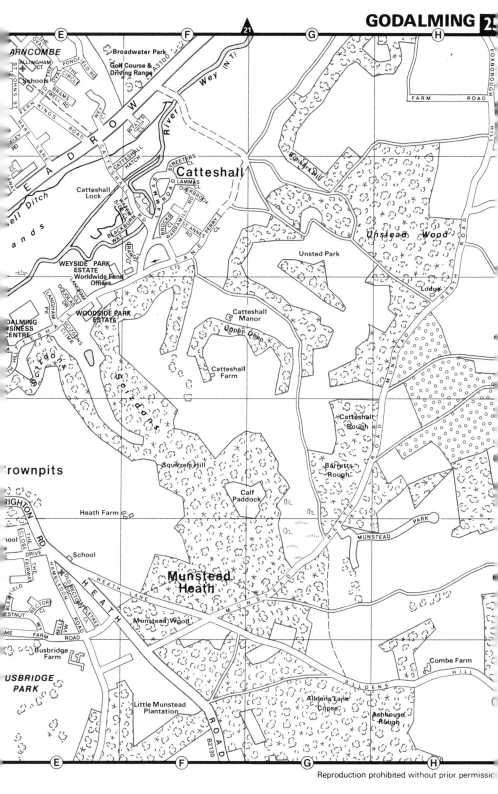

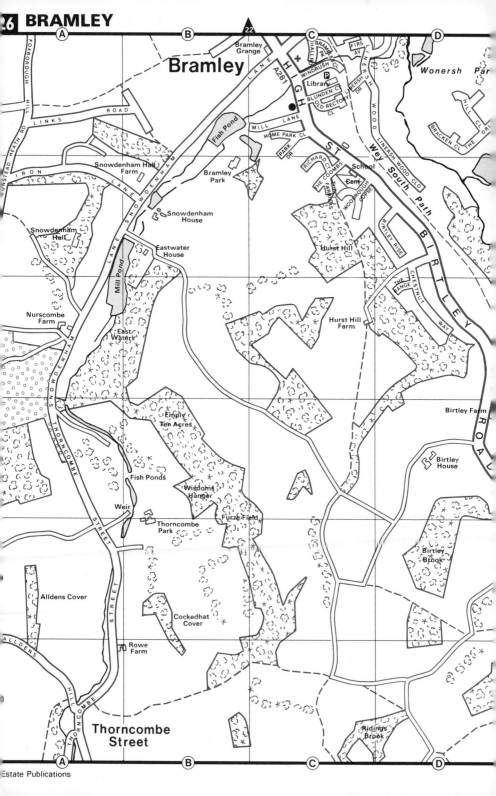

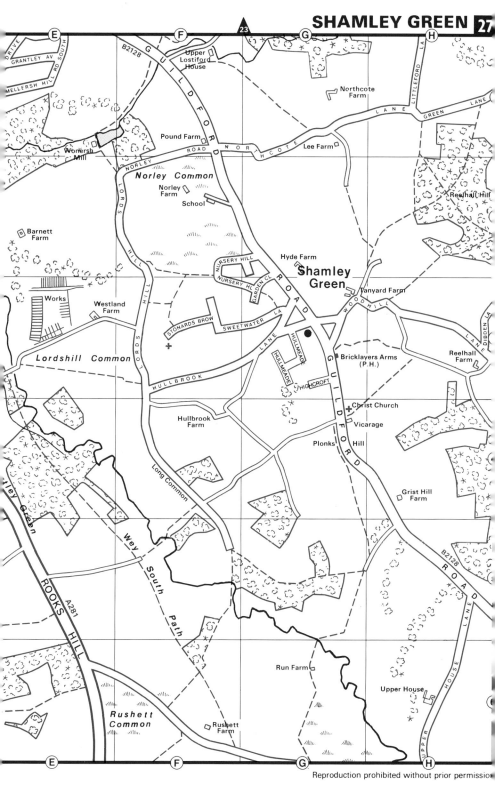

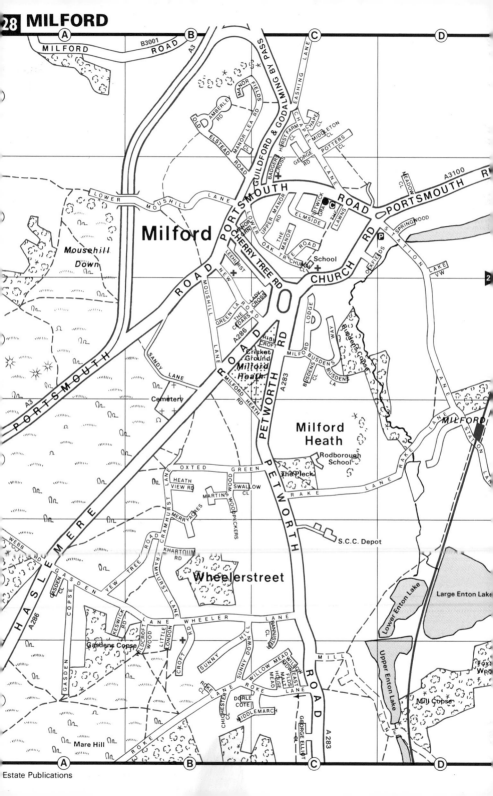

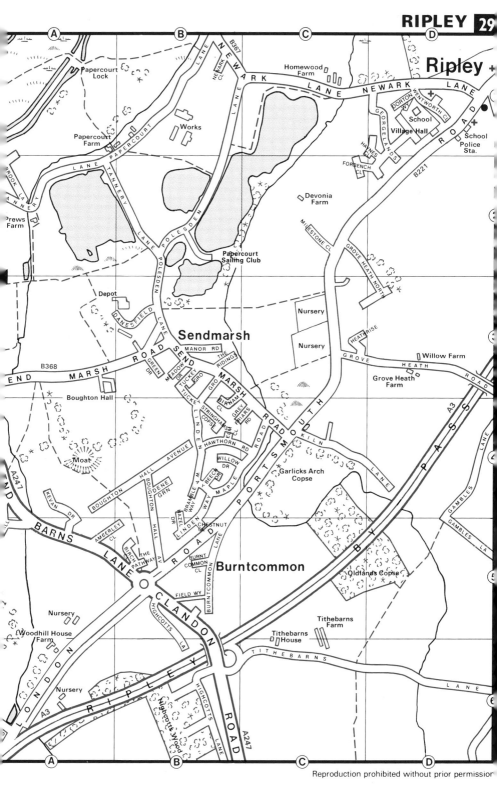

Ripley

Papercourt Lock

Homewood Farm

NEWARK LANE

NEWARK LANE

B367

School
Village Hall

School
Police Sta.

Works

DORTON
WENTWORTH CL
GEORGELANDS
HANES
FORBENCH CL

Papercourt Farm

PAPERCOURT LANE

TANNERY LANE

BROOK LANE

Drews Farm

POLESDEN LANE

Devonia Farm

B221

B221

MILESTONE CL

GROVE HEATH NORTH

Papercourt Sailing Club

Depot

DANESFIELD LANE

Sendmarsh

Nursery

Nursery

HEATHRISE

GROVE HEATH

Willow Farm

Grove Heath Farm

MANOR RD.

THE RIDINGS

B368

END MARSH ROAD

SEND MARSH ROAD

MEADOW DR

GREEN

TUCKEY GRO

TUCKEY CL

BIRNAM CL

STRINGHAMS COPSE

ELM GRO

GREY FRIARS RD

Boughton Hall

LINDEN RD

HAWTHORN RD

PORTSMOUTH ROAD

KILN LANE

Moat

BOUGHTON HALL AVENUE

BOUGHTON HALL

WILLOW DR

BRAMLEY WAY

BEECH AV

MAPLE

HAZEL

Garlicks Arch Copse

DENE GRN

AMBERLEY CL

KEVAN DR

BIRCH

THE PATHWAY

CHESTNUT

BURNT COMMON CL

A247

BARNS LANE

LONDON A3

Burntcommon

FIELD WY

BURNTCOMMON LANE

HIGHCOTTS LA

CLANDON

RIPLEY ROAD

HIGHCOTTS LANE

Oldlands Copse

A3 BY PASS

GAMBLES LANE

GAMBLES LA

Nursery

Woodhill House Farm

Nursery

Highcotts Wood

Tithebarns Farm

Tithebarns House

TITHEBARNS LANE

A247

A - Z INDEX TO STREETS
with Postcodes

The Index includes some names for which there is insufficient space on the maps. These names are preceded by an * and are followed by the nearest adjoining thoroughfare.

Aarons Hill. GU7 24 A3
Abbey Clo. GU22 8 A6
Abbey Rd. GU21 6 B5
Abbot Clo. KT14 9 F1
Abbot Rd. GU1 19 G5
Abbots Clo. GU2 18 C5
Abbots Way. GU2 17 G4
Abbotsford Clo. GU22 7 E5
Abbotswood. GU1 16 C3
Abbotswood Clo. GU1 16 C2
Abercorn Way. GU21 5 G4
Abingdon Clo. GU21 19 H4
Abinger Way. GU4 13 F5
Acacia Av. GU22 10 C2
Acacia Dri. KT15 8 B1
Acacia Rd. GU1 19 G2
Achilles Pl. GU21 6 A5
Addison Rd, Guildford. GU1 19 H4
Addison Rd, Woking. GU21 6 D5
Admirals Ct. GU1 16 D4
Agraria Rd. GU2 19 E4
Ainsdale Way. GU21 5 G3
Alan Turing Rd. GU2 18 B3
Albert Dri. GU21 7 F3
Albury Rd. GU1 16 C6
Aldersey Rd. GU1 16 C5
Aldershot Rd. GU3 14 A2
Alexandra Gdns. GU21 4 D4
Alexandra Pl. GU1 19 H4
Alexandra Ter. GU1 19 H4
Alford Clo. GU4 16 C2
Alice Ruston Pl. GU22 10 B1
Alison Clo. GU21 6 D3
Allden Cotts. GU7 24 B3
Alldens Hill. GU5 25 G6
Allen House Pk. GU22 10 A2
Allenbrook Clo. GU21 4 C4
Allingham Ct. GU7 21 E6
Alloway Clo. GU21 5 H4
Alma Clo. GU21 5 E3
Almond Av. GU22 10 B3
Almond Clo. GU1 15 H2
Almsgate. GU7 20 B3
Alpha Rd. GU22 7 F4
Alresford Rd. GU2 18 D3
Alterton Clo. GU21 5 G3
Alvernia Clo. GU7 24 C5
Amberley Clo. GU23 29 A5
Amberley Dri. KT15 8 B1
Amberley Rd. GU28 8 C1
Amis Av. KT15 8 C1
Amis Rd. GU21 5 E4
Amstel Way. GU21 5 F4
Anchor Cres. GU21 4 D3
Anchor Hill. GU21 4 D3
Anderson Av. GU2 15 F2
Angel Ct. GU7 24 C3
Angel Gate. GU1 19 G4
Angelica Dri. GU2 4 B1
Angelica Rd. GU2 15 E2
Annadale Rd. GU2 19 E5
Apers Av. GU22 10 D3
Applegarth. GU7 20 B6
Applegarth Av. GU2 18 A3
Appletree Clo. GU7 25 E5
Appletree Ct. GU4 17 F3
Aprilwood Clo. KT15 8 B1
Aragon Walk. KT14 9 G3
Aramethia Clo.GU24 4 A2
Ardmore Av. GU2 19 E1
Ardmore Ho. GU2 15 F4
Ardmore Way. GU2 15 F4
Armadale Rd. GU21 5 F3
Arnold Rd. GU21 7 F4
Arreton Mead. GU4 13 F5
Arthurs Bridge Rd. GU21 6 B5
Artillery Rd. GU1 19 F3
Artillery Ter. GU1 19 G3

Artington Walk. GU2 19 F6
Ash Clo, Mayford. GU22 10 C2
Ash Clo, Pyrford. GU22 8 C5
Ash Gro. GU2 18 D2
Ash Rd. GU22 10 C2
Ashbury Cres. GU4 17 E3
Ashcombe Par. GU22 11 E3
Ashcroft. GU4 22 B3
Ashenden Rd. GU22 18 C3
Ashley Ct. GU21 5 F4
Ashley Gdns. GU4 22 B3
Ashley Ho. GU7 20 D4
Ashley Rd. GU21 5 F4
Ashtead La. GU7 24 B6
Ashton Rd. GU21 5 F4
Ashwindham Ct. GU21 5 F4
Ashwood Park. GU22 7 E6
Ashwood Rd. GU22 7 E6
Ashworth Pl. GU2 14 D6
Aspen Clo. GU4 17 F2
Atherton Rd. GU21 22 B2
Atkins Clo. GU21 5 G4
Austen Rd. GU1 16 C6
Aviary Rd. GU22 8 C6
Avington Clo. GU1 19 H3
Avon Ct. GU1 16 D5
Avon Mead. GU21 6 B6
Avonmore Av. GU1 16 A3
Avro Way. KT13 9 F1
Azalea Ct. GU22 10 B1

Baden Rd. GU2 15 F4
Badger Clo. GU2 15 F4
Badgers Clo, Farncombe. GU7 20 C5
Badgers Clo, Woking. GU21 5 H4
Badgers Cross. GU8 28 C2
Badgers Hollow. GU7 24 C1
Bagshot Rd. GU21 4 B4
Baillie Rd. GU1 19 H4
Bainton Mead. GU21 5 G3
Baird Dri. GU3 14 A5
Baldwin Cres. GU4 17 F3
Balfour Av. GU22 10 D4
Ball Field Rd. GU7 24 C1
Balmoral Dri. GU22 7 G4
Bampton Way. GU21 5 G4
Banders Rise. GU1 17 F4
Banks Way. GU4 16 C2
Bankside. GU21 5 H4
Bannister Ct. GU8 28 C6
Bannisters Rd. GU2 18 D5
Bardon Walk. GU21 5 G3
Bargate Ct. GU1 19 H5
Bargate Rise. GU7 24 B3
Barley Mow Clo. GU21 4 D2
Barley Mow La. GU21 4 C2
Barnaby Rd. GU21 4 D3
Barnard Ct. GU21 5 E4
Barnato Clo, Dunfee Way. KT14 9 G2
Barnes Rd. GU7 20 D5
Barnes Wallis Dri. KT13 9 F1
Barnett Clo. GU5 23 E5
Barnett Hill. GU5 22 D6
Barnett La. GU4 23 E6
Barnett Row. GU1 15 H1
Barnwood Clo. GU2 18 B1
Barnwood Ct. GU2 18 B1
Barnwood Rd. GU2 18 B1
Barrack Path. GU21 5 F4
Barrack Rd. GU2 15 E4
Barrens Brae. GU22 7 E6
Barrens Clo. GU22 7 E6
Barrens Pk. GU22 7 E6
Barricane. GU21 5 H4
Barrisdale. GU21 7 H3
Barrs La. GU21 4 D1
Barton Rd. GU5 22 C6
Basset Rd. GU22 7 G4
Bateson Way. GU21 7 G2
Batten Av. GU21 5 E5
Battersea Way. GU2 18 B2
Beacon Hill. GU21 10 A1
Beaconsfield Rd. GU22 11 E2
Beatty Av. GU1 16 D2
Beaufort Clo. GU22 7 G4

Beaufort Mews. GU22 6 C6
Beaufort Rd. GU22 7 F4
Beavers Clo. GU2 18 C1
Beckingham Rd. GU2 18 D1
Bedford Clo. GU21 6 A3
Bedford Rd. GU1 19 F4
Bedser Clo. GU21 7 E4
Beech Clo. KT14 9 G2
Beech Dri. GU23 29 B4
Beech Gdns. GU21 6 C3
Beech Gro, Guildford. GU2 18 C3
Beech Gro, Mayford. GU22 10 C5
Beech Hill. GU22 10 C5
Beech La. GU2 19 H4
Beech Lawn. GU1 19 H4
Beech Way. GU7 24 D4
Beechcroft Dri. GU2 18 B5
Beechway. GU1 17 E4
Beechwood Clo. GU21 4 D3
Beechwood Rd. GU21 4 D3
Belgrave Manor. GU22 10 C1
Belle View. GU7 25 E5
Bellfields Rd. GU1 16 A3
Bellfields Ct. GU1 12 A6
Belmont Av. GU2 15 E3
Belmore Av. GU22 7 H4
Belvedere Clo. GU2 15 F3
Benbrick Rd. GU2 18 D3
Bentham Av. GU21 7 G3
Benwell Rd. GU24 4 A5
Berberis Clo. GU1 15 G4
Berkeley Gdns. KT14 8 B4
Berkley Ct. GU1 19 H3
Berrys La. KT14 9 F1
Beta Rd. GU22 7 F4
Binfield Rd. KT14 9 G2
Bingham Rd. GU2 15 F4
Binscombe Cres. GU7 20 D5
Binscombe La. GU7 24 C1
Birch Circle. GU7 21 E5
Birch Clo, Send. GU23 29 B5
Birch Clo, Woking. GU21 10 B1
Birch Gro, Guildford. GU1 15 G4
Birch Gro, Woking. GU22 7 H3
Birch Rd. GU7 21 E5
Birch Walk. KT14 8 C2
Birchanger. GU7 24 D4
Birchwood Dri. KT14 8 C2
Birchwood Rd. KT14 8 C2
Birds Gro. GU21 4 B4
Birdswood Dri. GU21 5 E5
Birnam Clo. GU23 29 B4
Birtley Rise. GU5 26 D2
Birtley Rd. GU5 26 D2
Bishops Wood. GU21 5 F3
Bitterne Dri. GU21 5 F6
Black Prince Clo. KT14 9 G4
Blackberry Clo. GU1 15 F3
Blackbridge Rd. GU22 10 B2
Blackburn Way. GU7 25 F2
Blackdown Clo. GU22 8 A5
Blackdown Clo. GU2 7 H4
Blackheath Gro. GU5 23 E5
Blackheath La. GU5 23 E5
Blackhorse Rd. GU2 4 D6
Blackmore Cres. GU21 7 G3
Blackness La. GU22 10 D1
Blacksmith La. GU4 23 F1
Blackthorn Pl. GU1 15 G4
Blackwell Av. GU2 18 A2
Blackwood Clo. KT14 8 D2
Blacon Mews. GU1 16 C6
Bladon Clo. GU1 16 C4
Blanchards Hill. GU4 12 C4
Blandford Clo. GU22 7 F5
Blencarn Clo. GU21 5 F2
Blenheim Clo. KT14 8 B3
Blenheim Gdns. GU22 5 H5
Blewfield. GU7 25 E5
Bloomfield Clo. GU21 5 E3
Bluebell Ct. GU22 10 B1
Blunden Ct. GU5 26 C1
Board School Rd. GU21 7 E4
Boltons Clo. GU22 8 C6

Boltons La. GU22 8 C6
Bonners Clo. GU22 10 D4
Bonsey Clo. GU22 10 C3
Bonsey La. GU22 10 C3
Borough Rd. GU7 24 C3
Boughton Hall Av. GU23 29 B4
Boundary Rd. GU21 7 E4
Boundary Way. GU21 7 E3
Bourne Clo. GU4 22 D2
Bourne Cres. KT14 8 D3
Bourne Rd. GU7 21 E5
Bourne Way. GU22 10 B5
Bower Ct. GU2 7 F4
Bowers Farm Rd. GU4 13 F6
Bowers La. GU4 13 E5
Boxgrove Av. GU1 16 C3
Boxgrove La. GU1 16 D4
Boxgrove Rd. GU1 16 C4
Bracken Clo, Woking. GU22 7 E6
Bracken Clo, Wonersh. GU5 26 D1
Bracken Way. GU3 14 D4
Brackendene Clo. GU21 7 E3
Brackenlea. GU7 20 C6
Brackenwood Rd. GU21 4 D5
Bradfield Clo, Burpham. GU4 16 C2
Bradfield Clo, Woking. GU22 6 C6
Bradford Park Est. GU4 22 A3
Braemar Clo. GU7 24 C4
Braeside. KT15 8 D1
Bramble Clo. GU3 14 C4
Bramble Way. GU23 29 B4
Brambledene Clo. GU21 6 B6
Brambles Pk. GU5 22 C6
Bramswell Rd. GU7 25 E1
Brantwood Dri. KT14 8 B3
Brantwood Gdns. KT14 8 B3
Bray Gdns. GU22 8 A6
Bray Rd. GU2 19 E4
Brewery La. KT14 9 G3
Brewery Rd. GU21 6 B5
Briar Clo. KT14 8 D4
Briar Patch. GU7 20 C6
Briar Rd. GU23 11 F6
Briar Walk. KT14 8 C2
Briar Way. GU4 17 E1
Briarwood Rd. GU21 4 D5
Bridge Barn La. GU22 6 B6
Bridge Clo, Byfleet. KT14 9 H2
Bridge Clo, Woking. GU21 6 B5
Bridge Mews. GU21 6 B5
Bridge St, Godalming. GU7 24 D3
Bridge St, Guildford. GU1 19 F4
Bridgehill Clo. GU2 15 F5
Brierly Clo. GU2 15 E4
Bright Hill. GU1 19 G4
Brighton Rd. GU7 24 D3
Brittens Clo. GU2 15 F1
Broad Acres. GU7 20 D5
Broad St. GU2 18 A1
Broadacres. GU3 18 B1
Broadford Rd. GU3 21 G3
Broadmead Rd. GU23 11 F4
Broadmeads. GU23 11 F4
Broadoaks Cres. KT14 8 D4
Broadwater. GU7 8 A2
Broadwater Rise. GU1 16 D6
Broadway. GU7 4 C4
Brockenhurst Clo. GU21 6 D3
Brocks Clo. GU7 25 F2
Brocks Dri. GU3 14 B2
Brockway Clo. GU1 17 E4
Brodie Rd. GU1 19 H4
Broke Ct. GU4 17 E3
Brook La. GU23 29 A2
Brook Rd. GU4 23 E2
Brooke Forest. GU3 14 B2
Brookfield. GU7 21 E5
Brookfield Dri. GU21 5 H2
Brooklands Rd. KT13 9 H1

Brooklyn Clo. GU22 10 C1
Brooklyn Rd. GU22 10 C1
Brookside Rd. GU1 15 H1
Brookwood Lye Rd. GU24 4 B6
Brodmcroft Dri. GU22 7 H4
Broomfield. GU2 18 B2
Broomfield Clo. GU2 18 C1
Broomfield Rd. KT15 8 D1
Broomhall End. GU21 6 C4
Broomhall La. GU21 6 C4
Broomhall Rd. GU21 6 C4
Bruce Clo. KT14 9 F3
Brushfield Way. GU21 4 C4
Bryanstone Av. GU2 15 E3
Bryanstone Clo. GU2 15 E3
Bryanstone Gro. GU2 15 E3
Brynford Clo. GU21 6 D3
Bryony Rd. GU1 16 D2
Buckingham Rd. GU1 16 C4
Bucks Clo. KT14 8 D4
Bull La. GU4 12 D2
Bullbeggars La. GU21 6 A4
Bunyard Dri. GU21 7 G2
Burden Way. GU2 15 F1
Burdenshott Rd. GU3 12 A2
*Burleigh Gdns, Grove Rd. GU21 7 E5
Burlingham Clo. GU4 17 F3
Burnet Av. GU1 16 D2
Burnham Clo. GU21 4 D4
Burnham Gate. GU1 15 H6
Burnham Rd. GU21 4 D4
Burntcommon Clo. GU23 29 B5
Burntcommon La. GU23 29 B5
Burpham La. GU4 16 D1
Burpham Rd. GU4 16 D1
Burrows Clo. GU2 14 D5
Burwood Clo. GU1 17 F4
Bury Clo. GU21 6 B4
Bury Fields. GU2 19 F5
Bury La. GU21 6 B4
Bury Mews. GU2 19 F5
Bury St. GU2 19 F5
Busbridge La. GU7 24 C4
Busdens Clo. GU8 28 C3
Busdens La. GU8 28 C3
Busdens Way. GU8 28 C3
Bush La. GU23 11 H6
Bushy Hill Dri. GU1 17 E3
Butts La. GU7 24 C4
Butts Rd. GU21 6 C6
Bylands. GU22 11 E1
Byfleet Rd. GU2 15 E3
Byrefield Rd. GU2 15 E3
Byron Clo. GU21 5 E3

Cabell Rd. GU2 18 B2
Caillard Rd. KT14 9 F1
Caledon Pl. GU4 16 D7
Calluna Ct. GU22 6 D6
Cambridge Clo. GU21 5 F4
Campbell Av. GU22 10 D4
Camphill Ct. KT14 8 C2
Camphill Rd. KT14 8 C3
Canada Rd. KT14 9 F1
Candlerush Clo. GU22 7 F5
Canewden Clo. GU22 10 C1
Canterbury Rd. GU2 18 C1
Capstans Wharf. GU21 5 F4
Caradon Clo. GU21 5 H3
Caraway Pl. GU2 15 E2
Cardamom Clo. GU2 15 E2
Cardigan Clo. GU21 5 E4
Cardingham. GU21 5 G3
Cardwells Keep. GU2 15 E3
Carlos St. GU7 24 D3
Carlton Clo. GU21 7 E2
Carlton Rd. GU21 7 E2
Carolyn Clo. GU21 5 F5
Carroll Av. GU1 17 E5
Cartbridge Clo. GU23 11 F5
Carterhouse Cotts. GU4 17 F2
Carters La. GU22 11 G2
Carthouse La. GU21 5 G1
Castle Hill. GU1 19 G5
Castle Rd. GU21 6 D2
Castle Sq. GU1 19 G4
Castle St. GU1 19 G5

*Catalpha Clo, Cedar Way. GU1 15 G4
Cater Gdns. GU3 14 D4
Cathedral Clo. GU2 19 E3
Cathedral Ct. GU2 18 D3
Cathedral View. GU2 15 E6
Catherine Clo. KT14 9 G4
Catteshall Hatch. GU7 25 E2
Catteshall La. GU7 24 D3
Catteshall Lane Link. GU7 24 D3
Catteshall Rd. GU7 25 E1
Causeway Ct. GU21 5 F4
Cavell Way. GU21 4 C4
Cavendish Rd. GU22 10 B1
Cavenham Clo. GU22 10 C1
Cawsey Way. GU21 6 D5
Caxton Gdns. GU2 19 E1
Cedar Gdns. GU21 5 G4
Cedar Gro. GU24 4 A1
Cedar Rd. GU22 10 A2
Cedar Way. GU1 15 G3
Celtic Rd. KT14 9 G4
Century Ct. GU21 6 D4
Chalk Rd. GU7 24 C2
Chancellor Ct. GU2 18 B3
Channings. GU21 6 C3
Chantry Rd. GU4 23 E2
Chantry View Rd. GU1 19 G6
Charterhouse Clo. GU7 24 D4
Chapel Clo. GU8 28 C1
Chapel La. GU8 28 C1
Chapel St, Guildford. GU1 19 G4
Chapel St, Woking. GU21 6 D5
Chapelhouse Clo. GU2 18 C2
Charlock Way. GU1 17 E2
*Charlotte Ct, Addison Rd. GU1 19 H5
Charterhouse Rd. GU7 24 C1
Chasefield Clo. GU4 16 D2
Chatfield Dri. GU4 17 F3
Chatton Row. GU24 4 A3
Cheapside. GU21 6 B2
Cheniston Clo. KT14 8 C3
Chequer Tree Clo. GU21 5 E2
Cherry St. GU21 6 C6
Cherry Tree Av. GU2 18 C3
Cherry Tree Rd. GU8 28 B2
Cherrytree La. GU7 20 C5
Chertsey Rd, Byfleet. KT14 9 F1
Chertsey Rd, Woking. GU21 7 E4
Chertsey St. GU1 19 G3
Cheselden Rd. GU1 19 H4
*Chesham Mews, Chesham Rd. GU1 19 H4
Chesham Rd. GU1 19 H4
Chester Clo. GU2 18 C1
Chestnut Av. GU2 19 F6
Chestnut Clo. GU23 29 B5
Chestnut Gro. GU22 10 D3
Chestnut Rd. GU1 19 G2
Chestnut Walk. KT14 9 F2
Chestnut Way, Bramley. GU5 26 D2
Chestnut Way, Godalming. GU7 24 D5
Chevremont. GU1 16 B6
Chichester Clo. GU8 28 B6
Chiltern Clo. GU22 10 B4
Chinthurst La. GU4 22 B2
Chinthurst Pk. GU4 22 B3
Chipstead Ct. GU21 5 E2
Chirton Way. GU21 5 G4
Chittys Walk. GU3 15 E2
Chobham Rd, Horsell. GU21 6 A1
Chobham Rd, Knaphill. GU21 4 B4
Chobham Rd, Woking. GU21 6 C4
Choir Grn. GU21 5 E3
Christchurch Way. GU21 6 D5
Christie Clo. GU1 15 H3
Church Clo, Horsell. GU21 6 C4
Church Clo, Milford. GU8 28 C2
Church Hill. GU21 6 B4
Church La. GU24 4 A1
Church Path. GU21 6 D5
Church Rd, Byfleet. KT14 9 G3
Church Rd, Guildford. GU1 19 G3
Church Rd, Horsell. GU21 6 C4
Church Rd, Milford. GU8 28 C2
Church Rd, St Johns. GU21 5 F5
Church St, Godalming. GU7 24 C3
Church St, Old Woking. GU22 11 G3
Church St East. GU21 6 D5
Church St West. GU21 6 C5
Churchfields. GU4 13 E5
Churchill Rd. GU1 19 H3
Chuters Walk. KT14 9 G2
Cinder Path. GU22 10 B1
Cinnamon Gdns. GU2 15 E1
Circle Gdns. KT14 9 G3
Clandon Rd, Guildford. GU1 19 H3
Clandon Rd, Send. GU23 29 B5
Clare Clo. KT14 8 C3
Claredale. GU22 10 C1
Claremont Av. GU22 10 D1
Claremont Dri. GU22 10 D1
Claremont Rd. KT14 8 C2
Clay La. GU4 16 D1
Claydon Rd. GU21 5 G1
Clayhanger. GU1 17 F3
Clayton Dri. GU2 14 D3
Cleardown. GU22 7 F6
Clews La. GU24 4 A2
Cliffe Rise. GU7 24 B4
Cliffe Rd. GU7 24 B5
*Clifford Manor Rd, Pilgrims Way. GU1 19 H6
Clifton Way. GU21 5 F3
Cline Rd. GU1 19 H4
Clinton Clo. GU21 4 D4
Clock House Clo. KT14 9 H2
Clockhouse Ct. GU1 15 G2
Clockhouse La. GU5 22 B6
Clover Ct. GU22 10 B1
Clover Lea. GU7 20 C5
Clover Rd. GU2 18 B1
Coachlads Av. GU2 14 D6
Cobbets Clo. GU21 5 H2
Cobbett Rd. GU2 18 C2
Cobbetts Farm. GU24 4 A1
Cobbetts Walk. GU24 4 A1
Codrington Ct. GU21 5 E3
Colburn Cres. GU1 16 D2
Coldharbour La. GU22 8 B5
Coldharbour Rd. KT14 8 B5
Coley Av. GU22 7 E6
College Hill. GU7 24 B5
College La. GU22 10 A1
College Rd, Guildford. GU1 19 G4
College Rd, Woking. GU22 7 F4
Collier Way. GU4 17 F3
Colliers Clo. GU21 5 H3
Collingwood Cres. GU1 16 D4
Coltsfoot Dri. GU1 16 D2
Colyton Clo. GU21 5 H4
Combe Rd. GU7 20 D5
Comeragh Clo. GU22 5 G5
Commercial Rd. GU1 19 F4
Commercial Way. GU21 6 D5
Common Clo. GU21 6 C2
Compton Heights. GU3 18 A6
Conford Dri. GU4 22 A3
Coniers Way. GU4 17 E2
Conista Ct. GU21 5 F2
Coniston Rd. GU22 11 F2
Connaught Cres. GU24 4 A6
Connaught Dri. KT13 9 H1
Connaught Rd. GU24 4 A6
Consort Ct. GU22 6 D6
Constitution Hill. GU22 10 D1
Coombe La. GU3 14 B1
Coombe Manor. GU24 4 B1
Coombe Way. KT14 9 G2
Cooper Rd. GU1 19 H4
Coopers Rise. GU7 24 B4
Copley Clo. GU21 5 E5
Copper Beech Clo. GU22 10 A3
Coppice Clo. GU2 18 B2
Coppice End. GU22 8 A6
Copse Clo. GU4 23 E2
Copse Rd. GU21 5 F4
Copse Side. GU7 20 C4
Coresbrook Way. GU21 4 B4
Coriander Cres. GU2 15 E1
Cornfields. GU7 21 E5
Cornwall Av. KT14 9 G4
Corrie Rd. GU22 11 G3
Cotts Wood Dri. GU4 13 E5
Court Green Heights. GU22 10 B2
Courtenay Mews. GU21 7 E4
Courtenay Rd. GU21 7 E4
Cow La. GU7 24 C3
Cramhurst La. GU8 28 B6
*Cranfield Ct, Martindale Rd. GU21 5 F4
Cranley Clo. GU1 16 D5
Cranley Rd. GU1 16 C5
Cranstoun Clo. GU3 15 E2
Creston Av. GU21 5 E2
Crobars Av. GU21 6 B3
Croft Rd. GU7 24 C3
Croft Rd. GU8 28 B5
Cromar Ct. GU21 6 A4
Cross Acres. GU22 8 B5
Cross Lanes. GU1 19 H3
Crossways. GU2 18 D5
Crown Heights. GU1 19 G6
Crownpits La. GU7 24 D5
Cubitt Way. GU21 4 D4
Cumberland Av. GU2 15 E2
Cunningham Av. GU1 16 D4
Curlew Gdns. GU4 17 G3
Curling Vale. GU2 18 D5
Cygnet Clo. GU21 5 H2
Cypress Rd. GU1 15 G4

Daffodil Dri. GU24 4 B2
Dagden Rd. GU4 22 A1
Dagley La. GU4 22 A2
Dairymans Walk. GU4 13 F5
Dale Vw. GU21 5 G4
Dane Ct. GU22 8 B5
Danesfield. GU23 29 B3
Daneshill. GU22 7 F6
Danses Clo. GU4 17 F3
Dapdune Ct. GU1 19 F3
Dapdune Rd. GU1 19 F3
Darfield Rd. GU4 16 D2
Dartmouth Av. GU21 7 G2
Dartmouth Grn. GU21 7 G2
Dartmouth Path. GU21 7 H2
Dartnell Av. KT14 8 D2
Dartnell Clo. KT14 8 D2
Dartnell Ct. KT14 9 E2
Dartnell Cres. KT14 8 D2
Dartnell Park Rd. KT14 9 E1
Dartnell Pl. KT14 8 D2
Dartnell Rd. KT14 8 D2
Darvel Clo. GU21 5 G1
Daryngton Rd. GU1 17 E5
Dashwood Clo. KT14 9 E2
Davies Clo. GU7 20 C6
Davos Clo. GU22 10 D1
Dawson Rd. KT14 9 F1
Day Spring. GU2 15 F2
De Havilland Dri. KT13 9 G1
De Lara Way. GU21 6 B6
Deacon Field.GU2 18 D2
Dean Clo. GU22 8 A5
Dean Rd. GU7 24 C1
Deanery Rd. GU7 24 C2
Deep Pool La. GU21 6 A2
Deeprose Clo. GU2 15 F2
Deerbarn Rd. GU2 19 E1
Deers Farm Clo. GU23 9 G6
Delta Rd. GU21 7 E4
Dene Grn. GU23 29 B4
Dene Pl. GU21 5 H3
Dene Rd.GU1 19 G3
Denholm Gdns.GU1 16 D2
Denmark Rd. GU1 19 G3
Dennis Way. GU1 12 C5
Denton Way. GU21 5 F3
Denvale Walk. GU21 5 G4
Denzil Rd. GU2 19 E4
Derby Rd. GU2 18 C2
Derrydown. GU22 10 A3
Devoil Clo. GU4 13 F5
Devon Bank. GU2 19 F5
Devonshire Av. GU21 7 G2
Dianthus Ct. GU22 6 B6
Digby Way. KT14 9 G2
Dinsdale Clo. GU22 7 E6
Dodds Cres. KT14 8 D4
Dodds La. KT14 8 D4
Donnafields. GU24 4 A2
Donne Gdns. GU22 8 A5
Dorchester Ct. GU22 7 F4
Dorin Ct. GU22 8 A5
Dorking Rd. GU4 23 F2
Dorlecote. GU8 28 B6
Dormers Clo. GU7 20 C6
Dorrit Cres. GU3 14 C4
Dorset Dri. GU22 7 F5
Dorton Way. GU23 29 D1
Douglas Clo. GU1 15 H1
Douglas Dri. GU7 25 E3
Dovedale Clo. GU1 16 D2
Doverfield Rd. GU1 16 C2
Dovers Mead. GU21 5 E2
Down La. GU3 20 A2
Down Rd. GU1 17 E5
Downer Meadow. GU7 20 D5
Downing Av.GU2 18 C4
Downs View Ct. GU1 15 G2
Downside Orchard. GU22 7 E5
Downside Rd. GU1 17 E6
Downsview Av. GU22 10 D3
Downsway. GU1 17 G5
Drakes Way. GU22 10 B4
Drodgers Clo. GU5 22 B5
Drummond Rd. GU1 19 F3
Duke St. GU21 6 D5
Duncan Dri. GU1 16 D4
Duncombe Rd. GU7 24 C5
Dunfee Way. KT14 9 G2
Dunlin Rise. GU4 17 G3
Dunmore. GU2 18 A2
Dunnets. GU21 5 E3
Dunsdon Av. GU2 19 E4
Durham Clo. GU2 15 E4
Dynevor Pl. GU3 14 B2

Eagle Rd. GU1 19 G3
Eashing La, Godalming. GU7 24 A4
Eashing La, Milford. GU7 28 C1
East Clo. GU22 7 G5
East Fields. GU8 28 C6
East Hill. GU22 7 G4
East Mead. GU21 5 H3
East Meads. GU2 18 D4
East Shalford La. GU4 22 A1
East Way. GU2 15 E6
Eastbrook Clo. GU21 7 E4
Eastgate Gdns. GU1 19 G4
Eastwood Rd. GU5 22 C5
Eaton Ct. GU1 16 D3
Echo Pit Rd. GU1 19 H6
Ecob Clo. GU3 14 D2
Eden Grove Rd. KT14 9 G3
Edencroft. GU5 22 C6
Edward II Av. KT14 9 G4
Effingham Ct. GU22 10 D1
Egerton Rd. GU2 18 C3
Egley Dri. GU22 10 B4
Egley Rd. GU22 10 B6
Elder Clo. GU4 16 C2
Eldor Rd. GU24 4 A1
Elgin Ct. GU1 16 C4
Elgin Gdns. GU1 16 C4
Elizabeth Ct. GU7 20 D6
Elizabeth Rd. GU7 20 D6
Elkins Gdns. GU4 16 D2
Elles Av. GU1 17 E5
Ellis Av. GU2 18 C4
Ellis Farm Clo. GU22 10 C4
Elm Clo. GU23 29 B4
Elm Clo. GU21 6 B3
Elm Ct. GU21 4 D3
Elm Gro. GU24 4 A2
Elm Rd, Farncombe. GU7 20 D5
Elm Rd, Mount Hermon. GU21 6 B6
Elm Rd, Woking. GU21 6 D3
Elm Tree Clo. KT14 9 G3
Elmbank Av. GU2 18 D4
Elmbridge La. GU22 10 D2
Elmgrove Clo. GU21 4 D4
Elmside, Guildford. GU2 18 D4
Elmside, Milford. GU8 28 C2
Elmstead Rd. KT14 8 C3
Elmwood Rd. GU21 4 D5
Elphinstone Clo. GU24 4 A6
Elsdon Rd. GU21 5 G3
Ely Pl. GU2 18 C1
Emmanuel Clo. GU2 15 E4
Emmetts Clo. GU21 6 B5
Englefield Rd. GU21 4 D3
Engliff La. GU22 8 B6
Ennismore Av. GU1 19 H3
Envis Way. GU3 14 A3
Epsom Rd. GU1 19 H4
Erica Ct. GU22 6 B6
Escombe Dri. GU2 15 F1
Europa Park Rd. GU1 19 F1
Eustace Rd. GU4 17 F3
Eve Rd. GU21 7 F3
Evelyn Clo. GU22 10 B2
Everest Ct. GU21 5 E2
Everglade Gro. GU4 22 B3
Everlands Clo. GU22 6 C6
Exeter Pl. GU2 15 E4

Fair Lawn. KT15 8 B1
Fairlawn Park. GU21 6 C3
Fairborne Way. GU2 15 F3
Fairbourne Clo. GU21 5 G4
Fairfax Rd. GU22 11 F2
Fairfield Clo. GU2 18 D2
Fairfield Rise. GU2 18 D2
Fairford Clo. KT14 8 B4
Fairlands Av. GU3 14 B2
Fairlands Ct. GU3 14 B2
Fairlands Rd. GU23 14 B2
Fairleigh Rd. KT15 8 C1
Fairmead. GU21 5 H4
Fairview Av. GU22 6 D6
Fairway. GU1 17 F5
Fairway Clo. GU21 5 G5
Falcon Ct. GU21 7 G2
Falcon Rd. GU1 19 G3
Falstone. GU21 5 H4
Faraday Ct. GU2 18 A3
Faris Barn Dri. KT15 8 B2
Faris La. KT15 8 B1
Farm Clo, Byfleet. KT14 9 G2
Farm Clo, Slyfield Grn. GU1 15 H3
Farm Clo, Fairlands. GU3 14 B1
Farm La. GU23 11 G6
Farm Rd (Foxborough Hill). GU5 25 H1
Farm Rd, Kingfield. GU22 11 F2
Farmhouse Clo. GU22 7 G3
Farncombe Hill. GU7 20 C6
Farncombe St. GU7 24 D1
Farnham Rd. GU2 18 A6
Farnley. GU21 5 F3
Farthings. GU21 5 E2
Fennel Clo. GU1 16 D2
Fenns Way. GU21 6 C3
Fentum Rd. GU2 18 D1
Fenwick Clo. GU21 5 G3
Fern Rd. GU7 25 E1
Ferndale. GU2 18 C1
Ferndale Rd. GU21 6 D4
Fernden Rise. GU7 20 D6
Ferndown Clo. GU1 16 C6
Ferney Clo. KT14 9 F2
Ferney Rd. KT14 9 F2
Fernhill Clo. GU22 10 B2
Fernhill La. GU22 10 B2
Fernhill Pk. GU22 10 B2
Fernihough Clo. KT13 9 H1
Fernley Ho. GU7 20 D5
Ferry La. GU2 19 F6
Field Clo. GU4 17 G3
Field Way. GU23 29 B5
Field Vw Cotts. GU7 24 B3
Fielders Grn. GU1 16 C5
Filmer Gro. GU7 24 D2
Finch Clo. GU21 4 C2
Finch Rd. GU1 19 G3
Finches Rise. GU1 17 E3
Findlay Dri.GU3 14 D2
Fir Gro. GU21 5 G4
Fir Tree Rd. GU1 15 G3
Firbank Dri. GU21 10 A1
Firbank La. GU21 10 A1
Fircroft Clo. GU22 6 D6
Firs Av. GU5 22 C6
Firsway. GU2 18 D1
Firwood Clo. GU21 5 E5
Fisher Rowe Clo. GU5 22 C6
Fitzjohn Clo. GU4 17 E2
Five Oaks Clo. GU21 4 D5
Flambard Way. GU7 24 D3
Fleetwood Ct. KT14 8 C3

t Catherines Pk. GU1 19 H4
t Denys Clo. GU21 4 C3
t Fillans. GU22 7 F4
t Hildas Clo. GU21 4 D3
t James Clo. GU21 5 G4
t Johns Clo. GU2 18 D3
t Johns Hill Rd. GU21 5 G4
t Johns Lye. GU21 5 F5
t Johns Mews. GU21 5 F4
St Johns Rise. GU22 10 A1
St Johns Rd,
Guildford Park. GU2 18 D3
St Johns Rd,
St Johns. GU21 5 F4
t Johns St. GU21 25 E1
t Lukes Ct. GU21 7 G2
t Lukes Sq. GU1 19 H4
t Margarets. GU1 16 C4
t Marthas Av. GU22 10 D3
t Martins Mews. GU22 8 C6
t Marys Rd. GU21 6 B5
t Michaels Av. GU3 14 B1
t Michaels Rd. GU21 7 G2
t Mildreds Rd. GU1 16 C4
t Nicholas Cres. GU22 8 C6
t Omer Rd. GU1 16 C6
t Pauls Rd. GU22 7 F5
t Peters Clo. GU22 11 G2
t Peters Rd. GU22 11 F3
t Thomas Clo. GU21 6 B5
alisbury Pl. KT14 9 E1
alisbury Rd. GU22 10 C1
alt Box Cotts. GU3 15 E1
alt Box Rd. GU3 15 E1
ampleoak La. GU4 23 G2
andalwood. GU2 19 E4
andfield Ter. GU1 19 G4
andfields. GU23 11 H6
andmore. GU23 11 H6
andpit Heath. GU3 14 B2
andpit La. GU21 4 C1
andringham Clo. GU22 8 C6
andy Clo. GU22 7 F6
andy La,
Farncombe. GU7 20 C6
andy La,
Guildford. GU2 19 E6
andy La,
Milford. GU8 28 B3
andy La, Send. GU23 11 G6
andy La,
West Byfleet. GU22 8 C6
andy La,
Woking. GU22 7 F6
andy Way. GU22 7 G5
anway Clo. KT14 9 G4
anway Rd. KT14 9 G4
appho Ct. GU21 5 E2
aunders Copse. GU22 10 A4
aunders La. GU22 10 A4
ayer Ct. GU21 5 E4
carlett Clo. GU21 5 F4
cholars Wk. GU2 19 E2
chool Clo,
Bisley. GU24 4 A1
chool Clo,
Slyfield Grn. GU1 16 A3
cillonian Rd. GU2 18 D4
cizdons Climb. GU7 25 E3
cotland Bridge Rd.
KT15 8 C1
cott Clo. GU2 15 E4
elbourne Rd. GU4 16 C2
elby Walk. GU21 5 H4
elhurst Ct. GU21 6 D3
ellars Hill. GU7 20 C6
elsdon Rd. KT15 8 C1
elwood Rd. GU22 11 F2
emaphore Rd. GU1 19 H5
emper Clo. GU21 5 E3
end Barns La,
Send. GU23 11 H6
end Barns La,
Sendmarsh. GU23 29 A4
end Clo. GU23 11 G5
end Hill. GU23 11 G6
end Marsh Rd,
Ripley. GU23 29 A3
end Marsh Rd,
Send. GU23 11 H6
end Rd. GU23 11 F5
eymour Pl. GU22 5 G6
eymour Rd. GU7 24 A4
hackleford Rd. GU21 11 E3
hackstead La. GU7 24 B4
hadyhanger Rd. GU7 24 D1

Shaftesbury Rd. GU22 7 E5
Shalford Rd. GU1 19 G5
Sheepfold Rd. GU2 14 D3
Sheeplands Av. GU1 17 E3
Sheerwater Av. KT15 8 B2
Sheerwater Rd. GU21 8 A2
Sheets Heath La. GU24 4 A5
Sheldon Clo. GU1 16 B6
Shelton Clo. GU2 15 E1
Shepherds Hill. GU2 15 E4
Shepherds La. GU2 14 D4
Sherwood Rd. GU21 5 E3
Shetland Clo. GU4 13 F5
Shey Copse. GU22 7 G5
Shilburn Way. GU21 5 G4
Shires House. KT14 9 G3
Shirley Pl. GU21 4 C3
Shores Rd. GU21 6 C2
Silistria Clo. GU21 4 C4
Silo Clo. GU7 21 E5
Silo Dri. GU7 21 E5
Silo Rd. GU7 21 E5
Silver Birch Clo. KT15 8 A2
Silversmiths Way. GU21 4 C4
Simmonds Cotts. GU7 24 A3
Singer Dri. GU23 11 G5
Slapleys. GU22 10 C2
Slocock Hill. GU21 6 A5
Slyfield Grn. GU1 16 A2
Smarts Heath Rd.
GU22 10 A5
Smith Ct. GU21 7 H2
Snelgar Rd. GU21 6 C6
Snowdenham La. GU5 26 A4
Snowdrop Way. GU24 4 A3
Somerswey. GU4 22 A4
Somertons Clo. GU2 15 E3
Sopwith Dri. KT13 9 G2
South Clo. GU21 6 B4
South Hill,
Godalming. GU7 24 D3
South Hill,
Guildford. GU1 19 G5
South Rd,
Guildford. GU2 15 F4
South Rd,
Woking. GU21 6 A3
South St. GU7 24 C3
South Vw. GU22 6 D6
Southcote. GU21 6 C4
Southway. GU2 18 B3
Southway Ct. GU2 18 B3
Southway Pk. GU2 18 D2
Southwood Av. GU21 4 D4
Sparvell Rd. GU21 4 B4
Speedwell Clo. GU4 17 E2
Spence Av. KT14 9 G4
Spencer Clo. GU21 7 G1
Spiceall. GU3 20 A2
Spinney Way. GU22 10 A3
Spring Clo. GU7 20 D5
Spring Ct. GU2 15 F2
Spring Gro. GU7 20 D5
Springfield Clo. GU21 5 E4
Springfield Rd. GU1 19 G3
Springhaven Clo. GU1 16 C5
Springside Ct. GU1 15 G5
Springwood. GU8 28 D2
Squirrel Keep. KT14 8 D2
Squirrel Wood. KT14 8 D2
Squirrels Clo. GU22 10 C4
Stafford Lake. GU24 4 A4
Stag Hill. GU1 19 E3
Stakescorner Rd. GU3 21 E4
Staniland Dri. KT13 9 H1
Stanley Rd. GU21 6 D5
Stantons Wharf. GU5 22 C6
Star La. GU22 10 B1
Starwood Clo. KT14 8 D1
Station App,
Godalming. GU7 24 C3
Station App,
Guildford. GU1 19 H3
Station App,
West Byfleet. KT14 8 C3
Station App,
Woking. GU22 6 D5
Station La. GU8 28 D2
Station Rd,
Farncombe. GU7 20 D6
Station Rd,
Godalming. GU7 24 C3
Station Rd,
Shalford. GU4 22 B2
Station Rd,
West Byfleet. KT14 8 C2

Station Rd,
Woking. GU22 6 D6
Station Rd,
Wbnersh. GU5 22 C6
Station Row. GU4 22 B2
Staveley Way. GU21 5 E3
Stewart Clo. GU21 5 F3
Stirling Rd. GU2 18 B3
Stockers La. GU22 11 E2
Stocton Clo. GU1 19 F2
Stocton Rd. GU1 19 F2
Stoke Gro. GU1 19 G3
Stoke Mews. GU1 16 A6
Stoke Park Ct. GU1 19 G3
Stoke Rd. GU1 19 G2
Stokefields. GU1 19 G3
Stonards Brow. GU5 27 F3
Stonebridge Fields.
GU4 22 A3
Stonebridge Wharf.
GU4 22 A3
Stonedrop Rd. GU4 17 F3
Stonepit Clo. GU7 24 B3
Stoney Brook. GU2 18 B2
Stoop Clo. KT14 8 D2
Stoughton Rd. GU1 19 F1
Stratford Pl. GU1 19 G6
Strathcona Gdns. GU21 4 D4
Strawberry Fields. GU24 4 A1
Strawberry Rise. GU24 4 A1
Stream Clo. KT14 9 F2
Streeters Clo. GU7 25 F2
Stringers Av. GU4 12 B4
Stringhams Copse.
GU23 29 B4
Studland Rd. KT14 9 G3
Sturt Clo. GU4 17 E3
Suffolk Dri. GU4 13 F5
Summerhayes Clo.
GU21 6 C3
Summerhill. GU7 24 C1
Summerhouse Rd.
GU7 24 C4
Summerhouse Rd.
GU7 24 C4
Summers Clo. KT13 9 H1
Summers Rd. GU7 21 E6
Summersbury Dri.
GU4 22 B4
Sundridge Rd. GU22 11 E2
Sunny Down. GU8 28 B6
Sunny Hill. GU8 28 B6
Sussex Clo. GU21 4 C3
Sussex Rd. GU21 4 C3
Sutherland Av,
Burpham. GU1 16 C2
Sutherland Av,
Jacobs Well. GU4 12 B4
Sutton Av. GU21 5 E5
Sutton Ct. GU2 15 E3
Sutton Green Rd. GU4 12 C2
Swallow Clo. GU8 28 B4
Swallow Rise. GU21 4 C3
Swan Ct. GU1 15 H4
Swan La. GU1 19 G4
Swaynes La. GU1 17 G5
Sweetwater La. GU5 27 G3
Sycamore Ct. GU1 19 H4
Sycamore Rd. GU1 19 G2
Sydenham Rd. GU1 19 G4
Sydney Pl. GU1 16 C6
Sydney Rd. GU1 16 C6
Sylvan Clo. GU2 7 F5
Sylvia Clo. GU24 4 B1
Sythwood. GU21 5 G3
Tamarind Clo. GU2 15 E2
Tamerton Sq. GU2 10 C1
Tangier Rd. GU1 16 D6
Tanglewood Clo. GU22 7 H4
Tangley La. GU3 14 D2
Tannersfield GU4 22 B4
Tannery La,
Ripley. GU23 29 A2
Tannery La,
Send. GU23 11 H5
Tansy Clo. GU4 17 F3
Tanyard Rd. GU5 22 B5
Tarragon Clo. GU2 15 E2
Tarragon Dri. GU2 15 E2
Tarrant Ct. GU2 15 F1
Teggs La. GU22 8 B6
Temple Bar Rd. GU21 5 F5
*Ten Acre,
Lockfield Dri. GU21 5 G4

Tenniel Clo. GU2 19 E1
Testard Rd. GU1 19 F4
Teviot Clo. GU2 15 E3
Tewkesbury Clo. KT14 9 F1
The Alders. KT14 9 E2
The Avenue,
Compton. GU3 20 B3
The Avenue,
Godalming. GU7 24 D5
The Bars. GU1 19 G4
The Beeches. GU5 22 C6
The Birches. GU22 6 D6
The Brambles. GU7 20 C6
The Broadway. GU21 6 D5
The Burys. GU7 24 D3
The Cedars,
Burpham. GU1 16 D2
The Cedars,
Byfleet. KT14 9 G2
The Cedars,
Milford. GU8 28 B3
The Chase. GU2 18 D3
The Circle. GU7 25 E1
The Cleeve. GU1 16 D5
The Cloisters. GU22 11 G3
The Close,
Godalming. GU7 25 E5
The Close,
West Byfleet. KT14 8 C3
The Close,
Woking. GU22 7 F5
The Close,
Wonersh. GU5 22 D6
The Coombes. GU5 26 C2
The Courtyard. KT14 8 C2
The Crescent. GU2 18 D1
The Dell. GU22 10 B1
The Drive,
Godalming. GU7 24 D5
The Drive,
Guildford. GU2 15 E6
The Drive,
Onslow Village. GU2 18 D5
The Drive,
Woking. GU22 10 A2
The Drive,
Wonersh. GU5 23 E6
The Fairway,
Byfleet. KT13 9 H1
The Fairway,
Godalming. GU7 25 E5
The Farries. GU5 26 C2
The Fieldings. GU21 5 F2
The Furlough. GU22 7 F5
The Gateway. GU21 7 F2
The Glade. GU21 8 A3
The Goldings. GU21 5 F2
The Greenwood. GU1 16 D5
The Grove. GU21 6 D4
The Hawks Nest. GU22 10 B5
The Hollands. GU22 6 C6
The Horseshoe. GU7 24 B4
The Lawns. GU8 28 C2
The Maltings. KT14 9 G3
The Manor. GU8 28 C2
The Meadows. GU7 19 F6
The Mews. GU1 19 F3
The Mint. GU7 24 C2
The Moorlands. GU22 11 E3
The Mount,
Guildford. GU2 19 F5
The Mount,
Woking. GU21 6 B6
The Oaks. KT14 8 C4
The Orchard,
Horsell. GU21 6 A4
The Orchard,
Mayford. GU22 10 D4
The Oval,
Godalming. GU7 25 E1
The Oval,
Guildford. GU2 18 D4
The Oval,
Wood Street. GU3 14 A5
The Paddock,
Godalming. GU7 24 D5
The Paddock,
Merrow. GU1 17 F4
The Pathway. GU23 29 B5
The Peacocks Shopping
Centre. GU21 6 C5
The Piccards. GU2 19 F6
The Pines. GU21 6 D2
The Quadrangle. GU2 18 D5
The Range. GU5 26 D3
The Ridge. GU22 7 F5

The Ridges. GU3 21 G1
The Ridgeway,
Brookwood. GU24 4 A5
The Ridgeway,
Guildford. GU1 16 D6
The Riding. GU21 7 F2
The Ridings,
Ripley. GU23 29 B3
The Ridings,
Send. GU23 11 H6
The Rowans. GU22 6 C6
*The Shambles,
Millbrook. GU1 19 F4
The Sheep Walk. GU22 11 G1
The Shimmings. GU1 16 D4
The Spur. GU21 4 B4
The Square,
Onslow Village. GU2 18 C5
The Square,
Wisley. GU23 9 G6
The Stables. GU1 15 H3
The Street,
Compton. GU3 20 A2
The Street,
Shalford. GU4 22 A1
The Triangle. GU22 10 B1
The Willows. KT14 9 G3
Thistledene. KT15 8 B3
Thorley Gdns. KT14 8 C4
Thorn Bank. GU2 18 D5
Thornash Clo. GU21 6 B3
Thornash Rd. GU21 6 A4
Thornash Way. GU21 6 A3
Thorncombe St. GU5 26 A6
Thornton Clo. GU2 15 E3
Thorpes Clo. GU2 15 E3
Thorsden Clo. GU22 6 D6
Thorsden Ct. GU22 6 D6
Three Gates. GU1 17 E4
Three Pears Rd. GU1 17 G5
Thrift Vale. GU4 17 F2
Thurlton Ct. GU21 6 C4
Thursby Rd. GU21 5 G3
Thyme Ct. GU4 17 E2
*Tilehouse Rd,
Pilgrims Way. GU1 19 H6
Tillingbourne Rd. GU4 22 B2
Tilney Gro. GU4 12 C4
Tilthams Corner Rd.
GU7 21 G5
Tilthams Grn. GU7 21 G5
Timber Clo. KT14 8 B4
Tintagel Way. GU22 7 E4
Tithebarns La. GU23 29 C6
Tolavaddon. GU21 5 G3
Tolldene Clo. GU21 5 E3
Tollgate. GU1 17 F5
Tormead Rd. GU1 16 C5
Torrens Clo. GU2 15 F3
Torridon Clo. GU21 5 G3
Tottenham Rd. GU7 24 D1
Tower Clo. GU21 6 B5
Town End St. GU7 24 D3
Town Sq. GU21 6 D5
Tracious Clo. GU21 5 H2
Tracious La. GU21 6 A4
Trebys Av. GU1 15 H1
Tregarth Pl. GU21 5 F3
Trenance. GU21 5 G3
Trentham Cres. GU22 11 E3
Tresillian Way. GU21 5 G2
Tresta Walk. GU21 5 G1
Trevose Av. KT14 8 B4
Triggs Clo. GU22 10 B1
Triggs La. GU22 10 B1
Trinity Rd. GU21 4 C4
Trodds La. GU4 17 G4
Tuckey Gro. GU23 29 B3
Tudor Circle. GU7 20 D6
Tudor Clo. GU22 7 E5
Tudor Rd. GU7 20 D6
Tuesley Corner. GU7 24 C5
Tuesley La. GU7 24 C4
Tuns Gate. GU1 19 G4
Tuns Gate Sq. GU1 19 G4
Turner Clo. GU4 16 C2
Turnham Clo. GU2 19 F6
Turnoak Av. GU22 10 C2
Turnoak La. GU22 10 C2
Twycross Rd. GU7 20 C6
Tychbourne Dri. GU4 17 E2
Tylehost. GU2 15 F2
Tyrwhitt Av. GU2 15 F1
Tythebarn Clo. GU4 13 F5

Ulwyn Av. KT14 9 G4

Underhill Clo. GU7 24 D4
Unstead La. GU5 21 H6
Unstead Wood. GU3 21 G3
Upfolds Grn. GU4 17 E1
Upper Edgeborough Rd.
  GU1 16 C6
Upper Guildown Rd.
  GU2 19 E6
Upper House La. GU5 27 H6
Upper Manor Rd,
  Godalming. GU7 24 D1
Upper Manor Rd,
  Milford. GU8 28 C2
Upperton Rd. GU1 19 F4
Upshott La. GU22 8 B6
Upton. GU21 5 G3

Vale Farm Rd. GU21 6 C5
Valley View. GU7 24 C4
Venton Clo. GU21 5 G3
Vernon Way. GU2 18 C2
Verralls. GU22 7 F5
Veryan. GU21 5 G3
Vicarage Gate. GU2 18 D5
Vicarage La. GU4 13 G2
Vicarage Rd. GU22 11 E3
Vicarage Walk. GU7 24 C3
Vickers Rd Sth. KT13 9 G1
Victoria Rd,
  Godalming. GU7 24 D3
Victoria Rd,
  Guildford. GU1 19 H3
Victoria Rd,
  Knaphill. GU21 4 D3
Victoria Rd,
  Woking. GU22 6 D5
Victoria Way. GU21 6 C5
Viggory La. GU21 6 A3
Viscount Gdns. KT14 9 G2

Waggon Clo. GU2 18 C2
Wakefield Clo. KT14 9 F2
Waldens Park Rd. GU21 6 B5
Waldens Rd. GU21 6 B5
Wallace Clo. GU3 14 B3
Walnut Tree Clo. GU1 19 F3
Walnut Tree Gdns
  GU7 20 D6
Walnut Tree La. KT14 9 F2
Walnut Tree Pk. GU1 15 G6
Waltham Av. GU2 15 F3
Walton Ct. GU21 7 E4
Walton Rd. GU21 7 E4
Walton Ter. GU21 7 F3
Wansford Grn. GU21 5 F3
Warbury La. GU21 4 C1
Ward St. GU1 19 G4
Warramill Rd. GU7 25 F2
Warren Hyrst. GU1 16 D6

Warren Rd,
  Farncombe. GU7 20 D5
Warren Rd,
  Guildford. GU1 19 H4
Warwick La. GU21 5 F5
Warwicks Bench. GU1 19 G5
Warwicks Bench La.
  GU1 19 H6
Warwicks Bench Rd.
  GU1 19 H6
Water La. GU21 4 A4
Watercress Way. GU21 5 G3
Waterden Clo. GU1 19 H3
Waterden Rd. GU1 19 H3
Waterers Rise. GU21 4 D3
Watermead. GU21 5 F2
Waterside Clo. GU7 25 F2
Waterside La. GU7 24 B4
Waterside Mews. GU1 15 G4
Waterside Rd. GU1 16 A2
Waterside Way. GU21 5 H4
Watersmeet Clo. GU4 13 E6
Watford Clo. GU1 16 C5
Watts Lea. GU21 5 G1
Waverley Ct. GU22 6 C6
Wayside Ct. GU21 5 E2
Wayside Park Est. GU7 25 E2
Waytrees. GU21 4 C3
Weald Clo. GU4 22 B2
*Wealdon Ct,
  Derby Rd. GU2 18 C2
Weasdale Ct. GU21 5 F2
Webb Rd. GU8 28 A5
Websters Clo. GU22 5 G6
Well Clo. GU21 6 A5
Well La. GU21 6 B5
Well Path. GU21 6 B5
Wellington Pl. GU7 20 D6
Wells Rd. GU4 17 E2
Wendela Clo. GU22 / E6
Wendron Clo. GU21 5 G4
Wendy Cres. GU2 19 E1
Wentworth Clo. GU23 29 D1
Wesley Pl. GU1 19 H6
West Hill Clo. GU24 4 B6
West Hill Rd. GU22 10 C1
West Mead. GU21 5 H3
West Meads. GU2 18 C4
West Mount. GU2 19 F5
West Rd. GU1 19 H4
West St. GU21 6 D5
West Way. GU2 18 C1
Westbrook Rd. GU7 24 B2
Westerfold Clo. GU22 7 G5
Westfield Av. GU22 10 D3
Westfield Common.
  GU22 10 D4
Westfield Gro. GU22 10 D2
Westfield Rd,
  Guildford. GU1 16 A1

Westfield Rd,
  Woking. GU22 10 C5
Westfield Way. GU22 10 D4
Weston Clo. GU7 24 D1
Weston Ct. GU7 20 D6
Weston Gdns. GU22 8 B6
Weston Rd. GU2 18 D2
Weston Way. GU22 8 A6
Westward Ho!. GU1 16 C3
Westwood Av. KT15 8 B2
Westwood Ct. GU2 14 D5
Wexfenne Gdns. GU22 8 D6
Wey Barton. KT14 9 H3
Wey Clo. KT14 8 D3
Wey Ct. GU7 25 E1
Wey View Ct. GU1 19 F3
Weybrook Dri. GU4 13 F5
Weybrook Park Est.
  GU4 13 F5
Weydown Clo. GU2 15 E1
Weylea Av. GU4 16 D2
Weymede. KT14 9 H2
Weyside Clo. KT14 9 H2
Weyside Gdns. GU1 19 F1
Weyside Rd. GU2 19 E1
Weyview Clo. GU1 19 F1
Wharf La. GU23 11 G5
Wharf Rd. GU1 19 F3
Wharf St. GU7 24 D3
Whateley Rd. GU2 15 F2
Wheatsheaf Clo. GU21 6 D4
Wheeler La. GU8 28 B5
Wherwell Rd. GU1 19 F4
Whipley Clo. GU4 13 F5
White Ct. GU2 15 E3
White Gates. GU22 10 D2
White Rose La. GU22 6 D5
Whitehouse Dri. GU1 17 E5
Whitehouse La. GU1 15 H1
Whitemore Rd. GU1 16 A1
Whitfield Clo. GU2 15 E3
Whitmoor La. GU4 12 B2
Whopshott Av. GU21 6 A4
Whopshott Clo. GU21 6 A4
Whopshott Dri. GU21 6 A4
Wilbury Rd. GU21 6 C5
Wilcot Clo. GU24 4 A2
Wilcot Gdns. GU24 4 A2
Wild Acres. KT14 9 E1
Wildcroft Wood. GU8 28 B5
Wilderness Ct. GU2 18 C5
Wilderness Rd. GU2 18 C4
Wilders Clo. GU21 6 A6
Wildfield Clo. GU3 14 A5
Wildwood Clo. GU22 8 B5
Wilfred St. GU21 6 B6
William Rd. GU1 19 F3
William Russell Ct.
  GU21 5 E4
Williams Walk. GU2 15 F2

Willow Bank. GU22 10 D4
Willow Clo. KT15 8 B1
Willow Dri. GU23 29 B4
Willow La. GU1 16 D4
Willow Mead. GU8 28 C6
Willow Meadow. GU8 28 C6
Willow Rd. GU7 21 E5
Willow Way,
  Byfleet. KT14 9 E1
Willow Way,
  Guildford. GU2 15 F2
Willow Way,
  Woking. GU22 10 C3
Willowmead Clo. GU21 5 G2
Wilson Way. GU21 6 B4
Windgates. GU4 17 E3
Windrush Clo. GU5 26 C1
Winds Ridge. GU4 13 G1
Windsor Clo. GU2 18 C4
Windsor Way. GU22 7 G4
Windy Wood. GU7 24 C5
Winern Glebe. KT14 9 F3
Winnington Way. GU21 5 H4
Winston Way. GU22 11 F2
Winterhill Way. GU4 17 E1
Wishbone Way. GU21 5 F2
Wisley La. GU23 9 E6
Withies La. GU3 20 B2
Wodeland Av. GU2 19 E5
Wood End Clo. GU22 8 B6
Woking Rd. GU1 19 G1
Wolseley Rd. GU7 24 D2
Wolsey Walk. GU21 6 D5
Wonersh Common Rd.
  GU4 22 D3
Wood End Clo. GU21 5 G4
Wood La. GU21 4 D3
Wood Ridings. GU22 8 B5
Wood Rise. GU3 14 C4
Wood Rd. GU7 21 E5
Woodbine Cotts. GU4 22 B3
Woodbridge Hill. GU22 19 E1
Woodbridge Hill Gdns.
  GU2 18 D1
Woodbridge Meadows.
  GU2 19 E2
Woodbridge Rd. GU1 19 F2
Woodcote. GU2 19 E6
Woodger Clo. GU4 17 F3
Woodham Hall Est.
  GU21 7 F2
Woodham La. GU21 7 F2
Woodham La. KT15 8 A2
Woodham Pk Rd. KT15 8 B1
Woodham Pk Way.
  KT15 8 B1
Woodham Rise. GU21 7 E3
Woodham Rd. GU21 6 C3
Woodham Waye. GU21 7 F2
Woodhill. GU4 13 H1

Woodhill La. GU5 27 G
Woodland View. GU7 20 D
Woodlands. GU22 10 D
Woodlands Av. KT15 8 B
Woodlands Ct. GU22 10 D
Woodlands Pk,
  Guildford. GU1 17 E
Woodlands Pk,
  Woking. GU21 7 G
Woodlands Rd,
  Guildford. GU1 16 A1
Woodlands Rd,
  West Byfleet. KT14 8 B4
Woodlawn Gro. GU21 7 E
Woodman Ct. GU7 20 D
Woodman Ct. GU7 20 B
Woodmancote Gdns.
  KT14 8 C
Woodpecker Way.
  GU22 10 B
Woodpeckers. GU8 28 B
Woodrough Copse.
  GU5 26 C
Woodruff Av. GU1 16 D
Woodley Ho. GU7 20 D
Woodside Clo. GU21 4 D
Woodside Park Est.
  GU7 25 E
Woodside Rd. GU2 18 C
Woodstock Clo. GU21 6 C
Woodstock Gro. GU7 20 C
Woodway. GU1 17 E
Woodyers Clo. GU5 23 E
Woolsack Way. GU7 24 D
Worcester Rd. GU2 14 D
Worplesdon Rd. GU2 19 E
Worsfold Clo. GU23 11 F
Wyatts Clo. GU7 25 F
Wych Elm Rise. GU1 19 H
Wych Hill. GU22 10 B
Wych Hill La. GU22 10 B
Wych Hill Pk. GU21 6 B
Wych Hill Rise. GU22 10 B
Wych Hill Way. GU22 10 B
Wykeham Rd. GU1 17 F
Wyndham Rd. GU21 5 H

Yarrowfield. GU22 10 C
*Yellowcress Dri,
  Angelica Dri. GU24 4 B
Yew Tree Dri. GU1 15 G
Yew Tree Rd. GU8 28 A
York Clo. KT14 9 F
York Rd,
  Guildford. GU1 19 G
York Rd, Woking. GU22 6 C

Zinnia Dri. GU24 4 B1

Edition 116 L 06.01